A to Z of

Spring

Tracy Nelson Maurer

Rourke

Publishing LLC

Vero Beach, Florida 32964

www.rourkepublishing.com

PHOTO CREDITS: All photos © Lois M. Nelson except: Cover © EyeWire; page 21 © Tracy M. Maurer; pages 6, 7, 17 © Diane Farleo; page 22 © Lynn M. Stone; pages 23, 27, 32 © Micheal Maurer

Cover photo: Spring is full of the colors of new flowers.

Editor: Frank Sloan

Cover and page design by Nicola Stratford

About the Author:

Tracy Nelson Maurer specializes in nonfiction and business writing. Her most recently published children's books include the RadSports series, also from Rourke Publishing LLC. A graduate of the University of Minnesota Journalism School, Tracy lives with her husband Mike and two children in Superior, Wisconsin.

Acknowledgments:
The author extends heartfelt appreciation to the children, parents, teachers, and photographers who graciously participated in this project. Your enthusiasm made every season special!

Notice:
This book contains information that is true, complete, and accurate to the best of our knowledge. However, the author and Rourke Publishing LLC offer all recommendations and suggestions without any guarantees and disclaim all liability incurred in connection with the use of this information.

Library of Congress Cataloging-in-Publication Data

Maurer, Tracy, 1965-
  Spring / Tracy Nelson Maurer.
      p. cm. — (A to Z of seasons)
Summary: Presents an alphabet of spring activities.
  ISBN 1-58952-197-8 (hardcover)
  1. Spring—Juvenile literature. [1. Spring. 2. Alphabet.] I. Title.
  QB637.5 .M38 2002
  428.1[E]--dc21

                                                2002004341

Printed in the USA

w/w

SPRING

Spring means busy days filled with many things to do, or verbs, from A to Z. People clean their homes and work in their yards to welcome the new season. What can you do to help around your home or school this spring?

Aa

Air out the blankets.

Bb

Bring a bouquet to Mom.

Cc

Clean your room.

Dd

Dig in the dirt.

8

Ee

Empty the water buckets.

Ff

Fill the hummingbird feeder.

10

Gg

Give pets a treat.

Hh

Help clean the driveway.

Ii

Invite a friend to play.

Jj

Jab stakes for a garden.

14

Kk

Keep scrubbing!

15

Ll

Lather the dog.

16

Mm

Match the socks.

Nn

Nap after lunch.

Oo

Open the windows.

20

Pp

Play at the park.

21

Qq

Quietly watch the robins.

Rr

Recycle glass.

Ss

Sow garden seeds.

24

Tt

Turn over the compost.

25

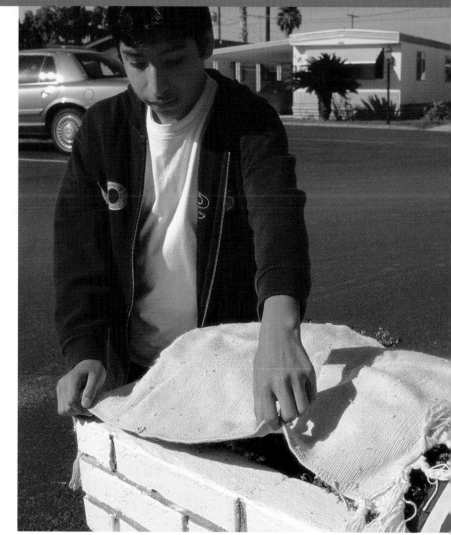

Uu

Uncover the flowers.

Vv

Vacuum the carpet.

Ww

Welcome back the birds.

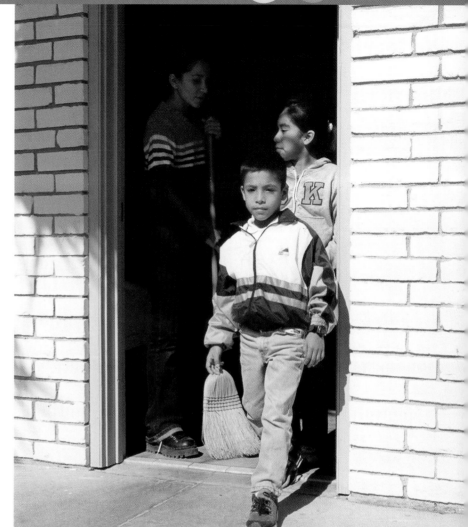

Xx

Exit while she sweeps.

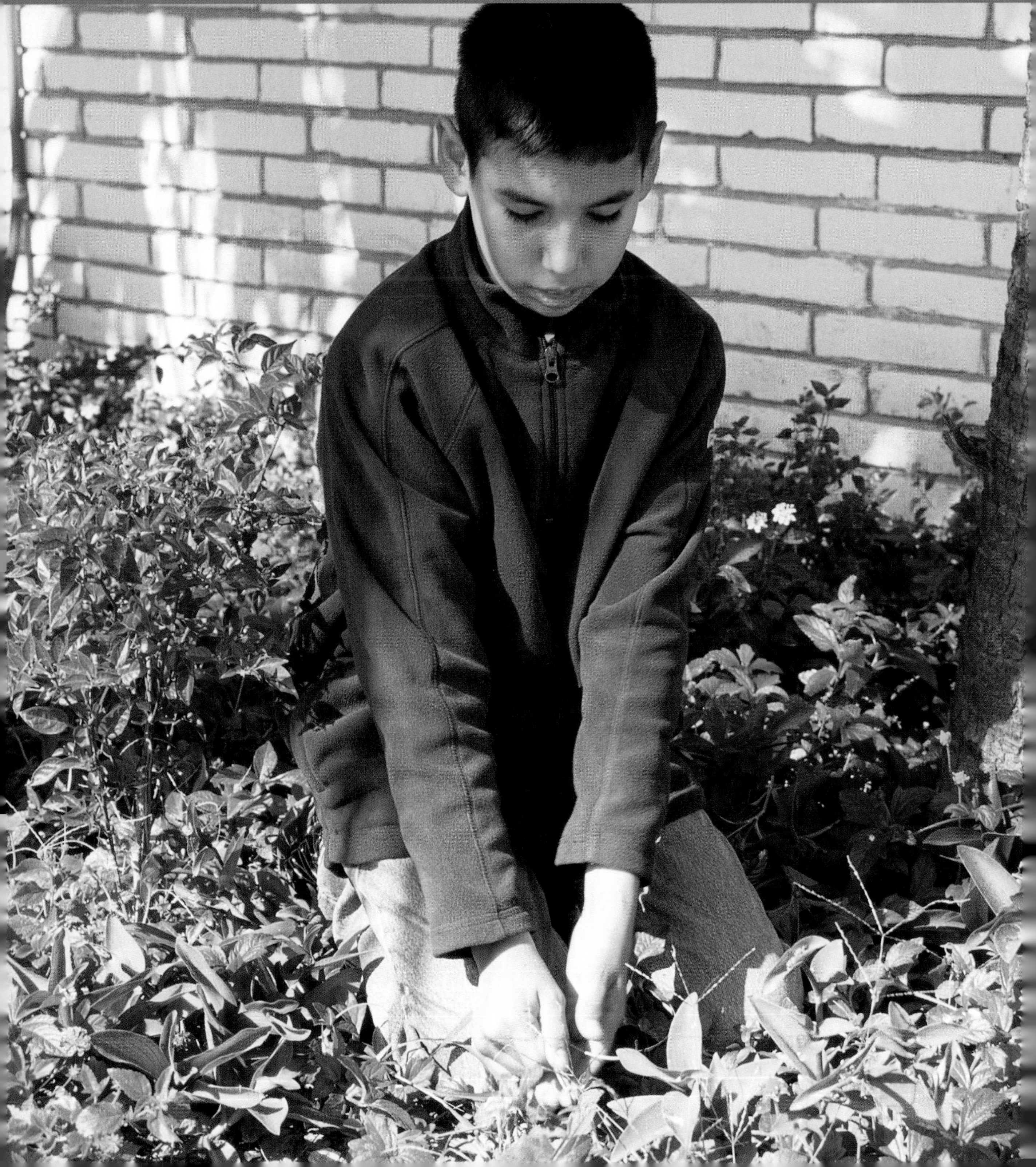

Yy

Yank out weeds.

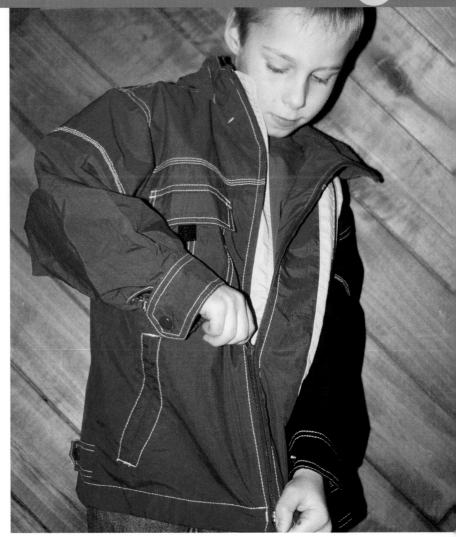

Zz

Zip up on chilly days!